Friction & Entropy

By

Christian Henderson

Friction & Entropy
Copyright: Christian Henderson
Published: June 2019
ISBN: 978-0-578-52954-7

ALL RIGHTS RESERVED. No part of this book may be reproduced or transmitted for resale or use by any party other than the individual purchaser, who is the sole authorized user of this information. Purchaser is authorized to use any of the information in this publication for his or her own use ONLY. All other reproduction or transmission, in any form or by any means, electronic or mechanical, including photocopying, recording, or by any information storage or retrieval system, is prohibited without express written permission from Christian Henderson.

This book was published with the assistance of Self-Publishing Relief, a division of Writer's Relief.

Cover design by Self-Publishing Relief
© Christian Henderson, 2019

TABLE OF CONTENTS

I'll Take Anything From You 1
Haiku in Quarters and Release 2
When I Think About You 3
Huguenot Cemetery 4
Agnodice (For Leilani) 5
The Sociology of Leisure 6
Damascus 8
Friction & Entropy 9
Gardener 10
Independence 11
For the One Who Should Ask 12
Flotsam 14
You Are Not My Sun 15
Specific Gravity 16
Taproot 17
New Orleans 18
Postcard Notes 19
Publix 20
1921 21
The Undertow of Forgetting 22
Afternoon 23
Autumn 24
Apples and Tells 25
Chicago 26
Two Nights in September—Five Poems for Her 27
Leaving 30

I'll Take Anything From You

I'll take any broken thing
As long as it comes from you
I'll take sticks and fallen feathers
Weathered shingles and rusty, twisted twine
I'll imagine an empty tube of glue
Worn-out guitar strings given a shine renewed
I don't need you to bleed
A selfless thought is all, indeed
But I would like to know it hurt you
Just a touch
I would like to know it hurt you
Just a little
To offer this part
Calloused a soft, sensate fingertip
A scissor slips
A week's worth of work comes apart
Or a corner of the green mosaic glass
Has a sneaky edge you discover
Pressing it into a frame you recovered
Maybe a little drop of blood does trail down
Falls to the floor under your feet
Becomes a puddle
A pool
An ocean
Drowns this conceit

Haiku in Quarters and Release

I only see worlds
I can hold within my wounds
The rest is ether

There is nothing left
Of me for you to consume
I am only bone

Watching you leave me
Is all the air in the room
An empty vacuum

I am content now
In my blood and bone cocoon
And my walls are tall

When I Think About You

When I think about you
(which is every day, every idle moment)
My insides are a vacuum bereft of blood receding
Into the cracks and dry bones of my desire

When I think about you
(which overcomes my other concentrations)
The moments like the times you looked up from the *Times*
Over your thin black glasses
Thick blankets on cold mornings

When I think about you
(which is still my last and first thought)
I imagine your sinewy openness wrapped around me again
In a borrowed bedroom
Where the clocks promised to stay stopped

When I think about you
(which is the best and worst part of surrender)
Every song, Impressionist painting, misty green Irish grove
Every battered Gulf seaside in the afternoon
All morning rain is your leitmotif

When I think about you
(which I know I shouldn't do)
I am the ocean surrounding an island
You are the light I will follow home

HUGUENOT CEMETERY

She is a crow
hanging over my shoulder
like a fine black point
an iridescent hidden green illuminant
in a darkness known by few
She bleeds a hint of bruised and broken blue
in a yellow fever St Augustine cemetery
where she made one from two

Her eye is a needle
numbing me in a remembered view
like a sigh
a bittersweet hue
wherein years and days have relentlessly forced me true
She is a promise of bruised and broken sleep
on a yellow fever St Augustine beach
where she made one from two

AGNODICE (FOR LEILANI)

In the faces of my child
Crying laughing somnambulant words
I see the birth of ages spent in other worlds
Entwined with warmth
From fires and friends
Keeping cold air foreign
Ears pressed against doors
Straining
Listening
For pauses bringing blessing
Supplanting sterility for human passion
She ushers in life
Slapping breath into lungs
Nine months dormant
The first other
To touch to hold
To enfold and wrap in warm arms
I imagine tears mingling
Connecting rivers from ages in pagan past
To the child who is new this night
In this
She is not other
She is Mother

The Sociology of Leisure

She is a liar
with nothing to lie about

So, I guess she is being honest with me
concerning the curiously
Dark
Long
Bewitching
hairs in the shower drain

I do not intend to mention them
as doing so would only move her
from the carefree
the indecent divot in the middle of the mattress

I have lost count
of the number of times she has said
I love you...
in the mornings
even in the evenings
during commercial breaks
when my presence
before the hairs
seldom stirred the slightest blush

Perhaps I should be subtle
inform her obliquely
in between the sentences
through notes scribbled about groceries:

we need milk or cat food...
Drano...
maybe hair gel...?

Yet I know
at least I suspect
I should scream from the impervious pedestal of virtue
point my finger
cry
vacillate from fury to forlorn concession

and do it all within the same rehearsed sentence
finally saying
between genuine spasms of anguish,
"I understand."

But that would be like washing the car in the rain

DAMASCUS

I've never held Damascus but I am her lover
I have tasted her earth
White stone skin almost as old as ourselves
Red bricks baked in a hot desert daze
Dusty
So much unrelenting dust it's impossible to hear other voices
Certainly, she is a jealous lover
All but the muezzin are silenced
His song of comfort and continuity
Echoes over the homes of the faithful
Curs and crows steal bread while children kick a football flat
Her midnight hair fills my senses with jasmine
As she moves over me like the moon
She is salty in the morning as I swim in her sea
She has pleased Alexander
She has lain with Lawrence
Lustful and lithe for her age
She tricks and contorts and I disappear into her secret waters
She will bend to the ruthless
She will rip open her heart for me
She will stitch it shut with the guts of her own people
I am in love with Damascus

FRICTION & ENTROPY

The easier thing to do
without sleep...
(The night
a series of broken promises of slumber
An uneven staccato like trains
on schedules almost kept
StartStop Start... Stop...)
The easier thing to do
is dwell on the destination
Fabricate a palliative comfort
a predilection for closure
Savor imaginary embraces on platforms unreachable
The harder thing to do
is discern the now barely visible embarkation
Transmuted by clouds of steam and smoke
The terminus ahead an apparition
Sleep
There is no desire
There is no desire
No desire
Sleep

Gardener

Dirt
Black and loamy
Pouring through your hands
The kernels of phosphate and nitrogen
Glisten in the earliest spring
When there is a promise that winter has gone from the land
Sunlit for now

INDEPENDENCE

Do you still read magazines
Do you ever smoke a cigarette
I picture you walking up stairs, looking up to the next landing
Your face alternating between light and shade with each step
In truth, I am behind you
Watching your hips sway back and forth
In a skirt I swear I think I bought you
Or maybe it was just the bracelet
Catching the dying rays of the Fourth of July sun
Both of which I know you only wear
When you know I'll be here
When will you stop bothering?
Maybe it's neither one
And you already have

For the One Who Should Ask

How to be human?
Listen to the progression of notes in "Ave Maria"
Or at least the lyrics in Danzig's "Mother"
Wrap your clean arms and clean shirt and clean heart
Around the dirty, forgotten other
Tell me you love me when it isn't true
Realize you're as ugly as the next
Smell your utter rottenness…if only in your shoes
Remember, the universe doesn't fucking know anything
She hasn't set aside a path or a road or a ditch for you
So you know a line or two
So you've done a line or two
Adamantly adhere to an agreeable or offensive thought or two
Only repeat it when you're sure
Sometimes
Most of the time
You'll still be wrong
Even that pleasure of becoming the other
Is enough to make you fall guilty into the pew
…and speaking of guilt…
Being human is diving in
Time and time, night and night
Again and again
I tell you, in truth, that's all right
The best years touch you in places
Your hands get the dirtiest anyway
The best people hurt you with words and deeds and feelings
That make your heart crave
That poignant pain
Every…single…day
Your worst is not the bottom
Your best is overlooked and empty
And so very hard to produce
You are human especially as an object in a noose
Be intransigent when certainty's light is dim

Fuck or be fucked on a whim
Don't scream
Don't fight
Paint
Plant
Kill (live? love?)
Write

FLOTSAM

She doesn't know anything though she pretends to
She's lost control again and she thinks I'm a fool
She's scattered me around her like leaves and broken trees
Her hurricane has torn me to pieces
I tried to build a wall taller than the sky
Sometimes I even prayed to Jesus
He didn't listen, he never will
So I'll just fall away and sleep,
Searching in the dark, feeling around for things to hold,
Blind in the darkness, powerless again in the deep

Your ocean washes over me
I dig my toes into your sides
Your ocean washes over me
Your waves are higher than the sky

YOU ARE NOT MY SUN

There are many days when you burn me to the quick
There are times you hide behind clouds of
Anger or doubt or pettiness
...when your light is the only thing I crave
I grow because I stretch to reach you
To take your skinny handed heat and own it wholly as my own
I dream you naked through a pinhole
Wishing I could see all of you...
...though I fear the seeing would blind
Please be with me in the morning
Please go dark with me tonight
I will dream of you searing my heart shut

Specific Gravity

The only time I have felt calm
The connection curiously concrete
Clouds passing over an open field
The earth, wet as silk in the morning
The trees, like saviors
Arms raised
Ascendant
Delivering
Separating me from the summer's heat
The only time
Passed in the syncopated flick of the horse's mane
Flies shaken from his neck
For a moment

TAPROOT

this taproot is deep she says,
caressing her shears,
it slides easily through the concrete foundation
meanders through the aquifer
sends tentacles through tight tributaries
stretches along the sun-splashed stream
vines up through the ancient treetops
nearly becomes the sky,
shameful
the intention
is only
one
swift
cut

NEW ORLEANS

New Orleans is a hopeful outcome, an answer to questions of depth and meaning, it is an association, a memory, a shadow, an aroma, a smell, a fog of stink falling against a loud, grinding, electric, glass-fuse grid of garlic and fish and oysters and cayenne and roux and bay and shit. Whistles and shouts hardly turn its head, so many times with doubtless certainty it has been left for dead, but the workers keep working, the tourists keep paying, the buildings keep decaying into that reluctantly American gumbo of order and chance, at once the question of how to make it work and the answer laid open before us

Postcard Notes

You're angry
much angrier
when you've been drinking ABC vodka all day

Muttering and swearing
waving your hand in the air
like a bloated Socrates

Knowing nothing
of Athenian exile
and less of self-doubt

Never equivocate
despite knowing you failed
to understand the question altogether

Grandiloquent and verbose
pretending concern when
only emptiness is evident

Publix

I know I don't matter to you anymore
so I'm sending this already in a vacuum
I went through your city today
stopped at the Publix
looked left at Salerno
drove on south
drove on through
I stay in places you and I have called home
for a night or two
for a time
and my heart is sometimes
well
Well
it is sometimes not ripped through
I'll pretend it's not now a rind
a hard half of itself
You'll move on and be fine
I'll move on and eventually be all right
You're a selfish girl
a defense I know you had to mine
And your looks left and drives south
are on different roads this time

1921

She was red and blue
   her paint is peeling
Flecking and cracked, rusting in the rain
Tortured and slowly turning
   someone like her I've seen
In a picture album
She's old and black and white
   more gray than any other thing
She's made of metal sinews
She's bone and broken skin
   next to me here sitting
   settling and maddening
I'll repaint her again and again

The Undertow of Forgetting

She walks
Struts, a queen
Drinking beers in brown-bagged cans
Stolen
Lean
Her fingers lost within those plastic collars
The oceans weave into a killing thing

Every word whispered in a secret scene
Each an invitation to her subtle appropriation
Of me
Her touch an epiphany
Her confidence a skinny moan
And me
Supine and serene

I want to feel her skin again
Rubbing languidly against mine
In a rhythmic lucidity
Entwined
Like everything isn't fantastical
Like everything is mine

Afternoon

There she lies
Her legs long
Loosely spaced
Neither apart nor one
Her cheek, warm
Fused to my lap by sleep
By trust
By proximal convenience
I feel I know I sense I need Her
In my bones
Every tiny red cell
Magnified
Suggests the same face I see pressed into me now

Autumn

Almost under your breath I heard you say, "I love..."
You didn't finish
I paused for a time I thought appropriate
Not too short so as to seem concerned
Not too long thus suggesting ambivalence
"What?"
You didn't answer.

We continued walking

I watched the leaves sinking onto the path before us,
Unrecognizable under its burnished blanket
.

APPLES AND TELLS

One day while making arrows with you I asked why our love is only platonic, why can't we dance to music both ethereal and spiritual, both corporeal and false, answering you looked deep into my eyes and said, oh, fletcher, long ago you missed the mark.

Chicago

It's cold in Chicago
On her crescent beaches in summer
And even on the hottest of days
Lake Michigan portends her chill
The aerials perched on darkened buildings
Are immovable even in her storms' furious mouths
Steady and rooted, unshakable
Though I sense she still does not know herself
Her deep and hull-pocked waters
Give her land its soul
And her tides change as if they are a sea

Two Nights in September – Five Poems for Her

Memories Are Laughter

You are beheld with eyes still and always new
which in all ways see only the beautiful in you
You are loved with a heart
which that beauty has crushed
It's been pierced with arrows and cold
both thoughtless and controlled
Its memories are laughter and ashes
everything you've touched

Well Those Passions Read

I would die in the desert in a day
Desiccated and evaporating
Lone and level with the earthly bed
Wishing at least the memory of you could hold my head

The Only Star

There is no firm ground
Terra firma
The intractable sands shift and coalesce
Into barbarous shapes
Digress into threatening winds
That clog once-bright eyes with their slow, erosional mischief

There is no limpid pool
Dame du lac
The waters move with the alacrity

Of old men to their chores
And smell of the city
Regressing
From its temporary exorcism
Once its sun has turned the corner in haste

There is only her

Violet by a mossy stone
Dwelling among the untrodden
So I too once knew her ways
And half hidden,
Although I'd hoped
From all but me,
I pray for a glance backward as she turns the corner in haste

Two Nights in September

There is an elegance to you
That belies your baser nature
Your hands
Delicate
Small
Utterly feminine
Pouring prosecco at nine in the morning
Sake at noon over wanton glances
(the unspoken anticipation
that pure and potent consummation)
Those recherché fingers de-stemming the herb
(Jiffy Pop
Tom and Tilda
Kiss Me Kiss Me Kiss Me)
Lovers at last
Asleep beneath a soft and blissful hum
For two nights in September

June 3rd - 4:51 a.m.

It's June...
and I haven't touched or seen you since Thanksgiving

Leaving

You're leaving all the evidence
that you were here
from your smell
to your music
to messy bedsheets
to your hair
C'mere, baby
C'mon back
C'mere, baby
C'mere

www.ingramcontent.com/pod-product-compliance
Lightning Source LLC
Chambersburg PA
CBHW031439040426
42444CB00006B/893